I0187820

The Holistic Voice

writings from the archives of

JAMES R. MCDONALD

compiled and annotated by

RUTH ANN MCDONALD

The Holistic Voice

The Holistic Voice

Writings on the rudiments of

BEAUTIFUL SINGING

from the archives of

Dr. JAMES R. MCDONALD

A tribute to him and his teachings,

compiled and annotated by

Dr. RUTH ANN MCDONALD

Printed in the United States
First Printing, 2022

ISBN: 978-0-578-92917-0 (Hardback)

Published by:
AnnieMcD Press
Loveland, Colorado

For our children,

Stuart Winston and Megan Marie,

who, as youngsters, patiently endured sitting through endless opera rehearsals and performances, recitals, Saturday morning voice lessons in our music room, which was just below their bedrooms, but who nevertheless grew into wonderful, music-loving adults with their own distinct interests and strengths,

Love always.

PREFACE

This book sets forth glimpses into the life-long journey lived by a man who grew to became a truly remarkable teacher of singing. It contains his musings, which he called *nuggets,* on the art of teaching voice students how to sing freely and beautifully, using a holistic approach to develop the total instrument of body, mind, spirit, and voice.

Based upon a thorough knowledge of the mechanics of the vocal instrument, James McDonald used imagery in his teaching. He inspired his students to develop a trust in what their minds and bodies could do to discover and facilitate the expression of their own personalities and their own unique vocal sounds and characteristics.

The human voice
is the
most beautiful instrument
of all,

but it is the
most difficult
to play.

Richard Strauss

Contents

Preface 9

____ The Back Story ____ 17

Introduction 18

Legacies 21
Britten Beginnings 22
Fateful First Meeting 23
The Croziers, et al. 26
Jim and Herald Stark 28
Prof. Stark's Observations 30
Jim and Poetry 35
Musings 37
About Musings 39
Requirements for a Singing Career 40
Mission Statement Easter '95 42
Goals for Students 44
Spring 1999 45
Studio Expectations Fall 2002 46
May 2008 48

____ The Nuggets ____ 53

About Nuggets 54
Golden Rule of Singing 57
In General 58
Technique 62
Repertoire Choices 68
Musicianship 69
Practice 72
Resonance 74
Diction 75
Study with Peter Pears 78

____ Addendum ____ 81

Biographies 83
James McDonald 84
Annie McDonald 85
Email to Students 86
Postscript 89
William S. Brady's Letters 90
Comments from Students 92
Josh Whitener 93
Mark Whitmire 96
Benjamin Czarnota 99
Gordon Hawkins 102
Susan Bender 104
Rachel Eve Holmes 107
Emily Hindrichs 110

____ Acknowledgements ____ 112

____ Photographs ____

Jim 15, 89
Jim and Peter Pears 25
Eric and Nancy Crozier 26
Jim and Herald Stark 28
Colorado Summer Retreat 43
Jim and Gordon Hawkins 49
Teaching at Middlebury 50
Middlebury Students 51
Indiana U. Students 52
Jim and Annie 83
Jim and Josh Whitener 92
Jim and Rachel Eve Holmes 106

____ Afterword ____ 114

JAMES RAY MCDONALD

1940-2011

Learning to sing is hard work requiring tremendous patience, persistence, and the right balance between freedom and discipline. But please remember that you all are pursuing this career because you love it. Don't let the hard work outweigh your love!

This is your future you are building. I am delighted to be a part of your lives for a short time and to guide and help you achieve your goals and dreams.

THE BACK STORY

INTRODUCTION

Jim's early childhood years were spent in Sibley, a small farming town of 2,700 in Northwest Iowa where his dad drove a Coca Cola delivery truck. By the time he started school, his parents were operating a small general store in Cloverdale, a tiny town not far from Sibley. Eventually his dad became a butcher and grocery store owner and the family, which now included his two sisters, moved back to Sibley.

He was always grateful to have grown up in that small-town environment, as it gave him a solid family life, Sunday morning church, good schooling, music instruction, team sports to play, and generally an opportunity to do his best in so many ways.

Throughout his life he was an incessant note writer, making lists of things to do, thoughts about particular students, what to work on in upcoming lessons, wise words to share with family, friends and students, goals for his own life ... the list of lists goes on and on.

What riches he gave us all—beautiful, heartfelt singing, great wit and humor, kindness, gentleness, caring, thoughtfulness.

When he passed away in 2011, I gathered up the many books, the music scores, the almost endless papers and spiral-bound notebooks from his office, and stowed them away to be dealt with at some later date.

Eventually I gave many of his books and scores to friends and former students. I encapsulated the story of his life for our children's future enjoyment in a set of six black binders, stuffed with papers, letters, and concert programs, reminders of the forty-three years of his performing and teaching careers.

But that left the issue of the amazingly copious supply of notes and annotations he had written about teaching voice. Those I put in a box, thinking that one day I'd like to do something with them—something that might be of value to future students and teachers. That day came in the form of the isolation imposed upon our world by the Covid-19 virus.

In these months of aloneness, the box of treasures beckoned. Hence, with the time and inclination finally given to dealing with his papers, I offer you this compendium of his written musings, prefaced with observations about his life and the learning experiences that contributed to his becoming someone who offered so much to the people and students who knew and worked with him.

Annie McDonald,
October 2021

THE LEGACIES

Teachers

Mentors

Friends

Britten

Pears

Croziers

Raridon

Stark

Brady

THE BRITTEN BEGINNINGS

In his undergraduate days at Morningside College in Sioux City, Iowa, Jim's voice teacher was Dr. Wade Raridon, who had previously studied with Herald Stark at the University of Iowa. Prof. Stark first introduced Dr. Raridon to the book *Vocal Wisdom* by Giovanni Battista Lamperti, who then introduced that treasured book to Jim. It was also Wade Raridon who told us about the music of Benjamin Britten, which ultimately became a primary focus of Jim's performing career. For his junior recital in 1961, we prepared Britten's *On This Island,* five songs set to poems by W.H. Auden. Also on that recital, we performed "Adelaide" of Beethoven, a beginning of Jim's great devotion to the German language and German art song.

On countless voice recitals throughout his performing career, Jim programmed German Lieder and Britten's songs and song cycles composed for the tenor voice. While teaching at the University of Maryland, he organized an extraordinary Britten Festival, with guest lecturers from here and abroad and performances by university faculty and students, culminating in the Maryland Opera Studio's presentation of Britten's opera *Turn of the Screw.* In addition to singing the role of Peter Quint in *Turn of the Screw,* Jim had previously sung the title roles in *Albert Herring* and *Saint Nicholas*, and

Nocturne with orchestra. He also wrote and performed two "Entertainments" with unusual formats, featuring German Lieder, American art song, and Britten's song cycle *Who Are These Children.*

Britten composed a great portion of his many vocal compositions for the tenor, Sir Peter Pears. They lived in Aldeburgh, a small fishing village on the English Channel. With the collaboration of director/librettist Eric Crozier, they founded the Aldeburgh Festival, and eventually the Britten-Pears School for Advanced Musical Studies, where Jim spent three summers as a student of Peter Pears.

A FATEFUL FIRST MEETING

In February of 1976, Peter Pears (not yet "Sir Peter Pears") came to Chicago, Illinois, to sing in Stravinsky's *Oedipus Rex* with Sir George Solti and the Chicago Symphony Orchestra. While there, he gave two master classes at Northwestern University. At that time, Jim was teaching at Millikin University in Decatur, Illinois, and applied to sing in one of the classes. Thrilled to be accepted, he chose to sing *Still Falls the Rain*, Britten's *Canticle III* for tenor, French horn, and piano. Not having a capable hornist at the time, we decided I should make my own reduction of the piano and horn interludes. As I think back on it now, I'm amazed at the naiveté of our doing that, an example of the old adage, ignorance is bliss.

As we stood to perform in the class, Peter very kindly asked, "Where is your hornist?" I blithely said we didn't have one and I had made an arrangement of both parts. You can imagine the incredulous look on Peter's face. Nevertheless, perform it we did. Silence ensued afterwards for many seconds. And then Peter stood and said ... as reported in the next day's *Chicago Daily News*, on February 3, 1976, by reviewer Karen Monson:

> He gave one student, tenor James McDonald, very high praise, when he promised to report on the young man's interpretation of *Still Falls the Rain* to Britten himself. "That's the way to approach it" said Pears. "Quite exceptional. I'm moved and delighted."

This wondrous encounter with Sir Peter was the beginning of Jim's three summers of study with him and others at the Britten-Pears School of Advanced Musical Studies in Aldeburgh, England. Over the years Jim sent a number of his own students to the school's summer courses, and eventually became a guest vocal consultant on a course there himself.

PETER PEARS

teaching

JAMES MCDONALD

At a master class in the Britten-Pears School of Advanced Musical Studies, Aldeburgh/Snape, England.

Summer of 1977

Asked to write his memories for the 35th anniversary of the Alumni Club of the Britten-Pears School, here are Jim's thoughts about those halcyon days of discovery:

"I was there as a student at the school in its earlier days. My connection came about because I was fortunate enough to sing at a Master Class with Peter Pears in Chicago. (I still have the score of the piece I sang, *Canticle III*, with his signature on it.) This led to his invitation to attend the school. Some of my fondest memories have to do with my meetings with him over the course of the three summers I was in attendance. He was a true gentleman as well as being a great, artistic singer.

Other memories include getting to know *Eric Crozier and **Nancy Evans, with whom my wife and I sometimes stayed when we were in England, and who visited us in the States on a couple of occasions. They became dear friends, and we remember with great joy our times at their home, Church Field Cottage, and later at 4 The Timberyard in Great Glemham. We also remember our sessions talking about and writing poetry with Eric. What great and generous souls they were. I was honored to be asked to be the American representative to speak at his memorial service in Aldeburgh after he passed away.

Eric Crozier, O.B.E.

Nancy Evans, O.B.E.

Other great memories were meeting John Shirley-Quirk and Gerhard Hüsch, both of whom were teachers on the courses in which I participated at the school. One interesting thing was that I had studied German Lieder with Gerhard Hüsch when I was in Munich on a Fulbright Scholarship.

The final memory I will share with you was meeting Felicity, Dowager Countess of Cranbrook, whose "small house" was just up the road from Church Field Cottage. Felicity was a devoted supporter of the Aldeburgh Festival and the school, and I was privileged to meet her and to stay in her home during one of my visits.

I can tell you also that my experience at the school, taking the classes and meeting the people I did (Roger Vignoles and Graham Johnson were two more) made a profound difference in my life, for which I will be forever thankful!"

**Eric Crozier's first collaboration with Benjamin Britten and Peter Pears was as director for the premiere of Britten's opera Peter Grimes at Sadlers Wells Opera Company in London, 1945. He founded the English Opera Group in 1947 and with Britten and Pears the Aldeburgh Festival in 1948. He wrote the libretto for Britten's comic opera Albert Herring and the libretto for his cantata Saint Nicholas.*

***Nancy Evans, mezzo-soprano, along with Kathleen Ferrier, premiered the role of Lucretia in Britten's opera Rape of Lucretia. Britten also composed for her the role of Nancy in Albert Herring, as well as his song cycle A Charm of Lullabies. She and Eric Crozier were married in 1949.*

One of Jim's students, Dr. Mark Whitmire, was also a student at the Britten-Pears School in Aldeburgh. Eric Crozier became an advisor for his doctoral dissertation. Mark tells about that experience on page 98 in the Addendum to this book.

JIM AND HERALD STARK

Jim studied with Professor Herald I. Stark at the University of Iowa for a total of five years—two years for his master's degree, from 1962-64, and three years for his doctorate, 1971-1974. When "Prof" retired to San Antonio, Jim and I would travel there on occasion for what I called "tune-ups," visits for lessons to check in with Prof vocally, and for chats about all things related to voice, teaching, and singing. These were special times. The two of them had a mutually respectful friendship, as evidenced by Prof giving Jim some of his own writings on voice along with copies of letters he had received from his teacher of many years ago, William S. Brady.

A discussion about voice between James McDonald and his teacher, Herald Stark, Professor Emeritus-Voice/Opera, University of Iowa.

Herald I. Stark (1907-1997) spent his childhood on a Nebraska farm, living in a sod house for several years. He was always surrounded by music. His father was an old time fiddler and his parents and siblings sang together for their church's special occasions. After receiving his Master's degree from the University of Iowa, he was the Director of University Choruses for twenty-five years, in addition to eventually becoming chair of the voice department. He taught at Iowa for 44 years, also conducting the summer operas and building an outstanding voice department.

Prof Stark says: "I am still mystified at what happens when someone opens their mouth and sings. Singing comes from the mind. I think thoughts are making it happen. Pavarotti says that before he sings a word, he has to think it. We sing what is in our minds—romance or anger, whatever we are truly feeling. We must respond to the tone or text of a song. The perfect singer does both."

The voice is an instrument that has not changed physically over the countless centuries people have been singing. Tastes in tonal characteristics may change over the years. And there certainly are different schools of thought about how to teach the art of singing. But for centuries the fundamentals of healthy technique for beautiful classical vocalism have remained essentially constant. Herein are some thoughts about singing from two "old masters," Herald Stark and *William Brady. Their wisdoms are as timely now as they were decades ago. *See p. 90 in thevAddendum.

Some Observations on Breathing for Singers

By Herald I. Stark

... I do wonder and marvel at the glorious sounds that come from the human throat. I wonder about musical talent and about our compelling urge to sing. I wonder about the various components of talent, the sense of hearing, the deep response to rhythm, and the gifts for communication and expression. I wonder about personality, charisma, intelligence, and the qualities that a singer must have to market his product. These intangibles are difficult to measure and certainly difficult to teach. As someone said to me, we do not teach voice, we teach people.

The vocal instrument is, basically, a simple wind instrument with a double reed buzzer in the throat which is enclosed in what we call the Adam's Apple. Above and below the larynx, the correct name for the "Apple," is a tube. The tube connects with the lungs, where air is stored. Air is taken into the lungs by the expansion of the ribs and the dropping of the diaphragm, which causes a slight protrusion of the abdomen. Air is controlled and forced out of the body by the contraction of the abdominal and intercostal (rib) muscles. We say that inspiration of breath is primarily a function of the chest while expiration of breath is primarily a function of the abdominal area. Above the throat are the resonators (throat, mouth, nose, sinuses, in fact the whole of the head) and the articulators. The resonators do as their name suggests. They amplify the sound. The articulators (tongue, lips, teeth, jaw, and soft palate) form the sound into vowels and consonants. The vocal instrument is, unlike mechanical musical instruments, flexible and capable of a myriad of varying sounds and pitches.

To make a simple sound, i.e., "ah," air is drawn into the body generally very quickly. No more than a sip. Some use the definition "a quick, snatched breath." To hold the breath, the larynx (vocal cords) closes. Breath is released against the cords and they open, close, open, close ..., vibrating until the air pressure is released.

We have little or no control over this part of our instrument. It is best not to think of its action. Speech therapists find, however, that singers are inclined to pitch their speaking voices too low; and some, particularly those with low voices, tend to seek too much laryngeal resonance, causing hoarseness and raspy tones. Since singing is an extension of speech, let us look at some approaches to breathing and support for the singing voice. As Lamperti said: "The foundation of all vocal study lies in the control of breath."

I find the most direct method of teaching breathing is in *Modern Techniques of Vocal Rehabilitation* by Morton Cooper. Cooper has the student or patient lie on his back on the floor with one hand on his chest and the other on his abdomen, breathing alternately through the nostrils and the mouth.

Breathing should be gentle and not forced. During inhalation, the stomach, or midsection as Cooper labels it, moves outward and comes in during exhalation. The chest remains stationary. When these movements become easy, the singer should sing a series of short notes in the easy part of his range. While singing from this prone position, the singer can quickly tell if he is tensing his midsection muscles unduly. If there is tension, the teacher should caution the singer not to make a fist of his stomach muscles. This is exactly what many do while inhaling and the muscles do the work instead of the breath. Next, practice the above in a standing position. The third and most difficult position is sitting.

... The late Kenneth Westerman, a voice scientist from the University of Michigan turned voice teacher, argued that without correct posture all breathing methods were futile. ... He contended that over 90% of all breathing problems could be traced to bad posture. "... breath control is the source of clear tones, clear tones are a distinct help in resonation, and full and resonant tones release the freedom of articulation.

In other words, freedom in articulation is impossible without full and free resonation; a fully resonant tone is impossible without that tone being clear and breathless; flexible, clear tones are impossible without proper breath control; good breath control is impossible without an alert and active posture."

Respiration, support, and management of the breath are, in my estimation, the foundations of a secure and lasting vocal technique. Without a disciplined technique there is little chance of the voice reaching its full power and beauty. From the great singers and teachers of the past to those of the present, the unifying thread is the same: breathe, breathe.

Mettete ben la voce,
Respirate bene,
Pronunciate chiaramente,
Ed il vostro canto sara perfetto.

(Place your voice well, breathe well, pronounce clearly, and your singing will be perfect.)
Gasparo Pacchierotti (1740-1821)

N.B. In this article by Herald I. Stark, a copy of which he gave to Jim, Prof Stark indicated that reference sources were three books: *Modern Techniques of Vocal Rehabilitation*, by Morton Cooper; *Vocal Wisdom*, by Giovanni Battista Lamperti and William Earl Brown; and *Emergent Voice*, by Kenneth N. Westermann.

In a letter to Jim on March 1, 1990, Prof Stark wrote: "You now are gaining a good understanding of breath management, which is not push or pull but an undisturbed sensation from deep in the groin area. Remember what we read in *Vocal Wisdom*. The voice starts and stops from the abdominal area; the muscles from the waist to the throat are concerned with resonance (power), and the larynx (vocal cords) are the pitch setters. Resonance is felt in the upper chest (low tones), the mouth, *and* the head."

JIM AND POETRY

While teaching at the University of Maryland for nineteen years, Jim had a sabbatical semester during which he took a university course in poetry. He had long loved and written poetry, which might help explain why he was enamored of the songs of Benjamin Britten and the German Lieder composers, because of the beautiful texts those composers chose for their song-writing.

Here is one he wrote years ago:

A POEM

Eagerly through the woods I go

Wand'ring a winding way,

Which leads to the banks of a turbulent flow,

T'wards the first star's shine I stray.

Darkness appears in the sky above

(One pellucid thought alone):

To follow the flight of the homeward dove,

Or press on towards the future unknown?

MUSINGS

Technique is not something
you superimpose on your voice;
it's a systematic approach
to the primal use
of your body and your voice.

About "Musings"

Always a quiet, thinking person, Jim had a regular habit of sitting at his desk every evening to prepare for each of the next day's lessons. In a three-ring binder he would have pages for each student where he wrote the upcoming day's goals, vocalizes they did that were productive, repertoire to work on, students' personal comments, and his own observations.

It was quite remarkable that former students came from far and wide to our little city of Loveland, Colorado, to attend, and some to sing in the beautiful memorial concert at Colorado State University. He nurtured not only the voice, but perhaps even more importantly—the individual.

As his awareness and understanding grew—of people's varied characteristics and needs—coupled with his continual study of the voice and vocal pedagogy, so did his requirements for himself and his students. Following are examples of his musings—what he would write as reminders of what he wanted to focus on in his life and in his teaching;

Requirements for a Singing Career

Mission Statement, Easter 1995

Musings: Goals for Students

Musings: Spring 1999

McDonald Studio Expectations, Fall 2002

Musings: May 2008

Musings: REQUIREMENTS FOR A SINGING CAREER

Having a singing career is a major undertaking, filled with great joy as well as frustrations and challenges. Jim had always known that he would ultimately be teaching. His voice and personality were such that instead of a career in opera, the concert and recital repertoire suited him beautifully. Thus he had countless wonderful performance opportunities during his long teaching career. He wrote this for his students:

"Following are attributes I would consider necessary if you wish to pursue a performing career. Hopefully this will prompt a continuous dialogue concerning your aspirations:

Perseverance

Productive attitude towards work

25 layers of thick skin

Self confidence, healthy ego

Fire in the belly

Healthy balance between work and enjoyment

Repertoire that suits your voice and personality

Physical "muscle tone;"

General

Vocal– Breathing

Language study

Musical study

Text study

Acting study (Opera Programs)

Vocal talent

Instincts

Personality!

Ability to work on technique but then to get beyond it—to use it. (You control it instead of it controlling you.)

Professional Connections

Luck

Dedication

Learning to sing is hard work, requiring tremendous patience, persistence, and the right balance between freedom and discipline. But please remember that you all are pursuing this career because you love it. Don't let the hard work outweigh your love!"

MISSION STATEMENT

Easter Sunday, April 16, 1995

This hung on the bulletin board over his voice studio desk.

—-I WILL SEEK TO EMPOWER PEOPLE-—

To live true to principles: charity, fidelity, self-sufficiency, honesty, integrity, proactivity, giving, trust, fairness, balance.

To give, then receive—to love, then be loved—to understand, then be understood—to bring healing, not disease— to enrich, not to be rich.

To use and stretch my strengths.

To treasure family and friends.

To treasure strangers.

To teach others, if they wish, what I know, and to learn what I can from them.

To recognize that I am not an owner of anything, but a steward.

To recognize that rights are much less important than obligations.

To be a light unto others.

To see each day as opportunity, excitement, and adventure.

To experience life with the awe of a child.

To begin each day with a smile.

To share my innermost thoughts.

To be interdependent—to develop shared visions.

To be responsive and responsible.

To stimulate daily mind and body.

To remember that without risk there is neither success nor failure. Thomas Aquinas: "If the primary mission of a captain were to preserve his ship, he would never leave port."

Never to react to abuse by passing it on.

Our soul-refreshing retreat in the Colorado Mountains

To find the self within that can and does look at all sides without loss.

To pursue excellence; to achieve respect and knowledge in order to help others.

To find win-win always; not to be willing to win at the cost of another's spirit.

Musings: GOALS FOR STUDENTS

1. "Discovery" learning stimulates imagination—which is different from "being told" learning.
2. "Treasure Hunts" instead of "Research Projects."
3. Must be taught to be independent.
4. Teach them to be unique—to develop *their* uniqueness.
5. Nerves—welcome them. Don't recreate the one time it was perfect; rather create something new!
6. "Imagination" is sometimes missing these days.
7. Teach "how to learn."
8. Build confidence in their strengths.
9. Teach to "reach beyond limitations."
10. Teach "make your own choices."
11. Develop them as artists and as people.
12. What is the desire in each person that drives them as a performer?
13. Feedback is important. Observations, not judgements.
14. Be a risk facilitator—mistakes help you grow.
15. Singers' backs—we tend to cut off this half of us because the audience is in front.
16. Interpretation begins from the depth of meaning of the words.

Musings: SPRING 1999

Value of systematic exercises and study:

1. Oren Brown's back breathing—"sniff" expansion—positions entire instrument and releases jaw and tongue, frees palate and back (stable body—stable larynx).
2. Whispered "ah."
3. Oren Brown's cricoarytenoid exercises on staff.
4. Consonant exercises. (How we pronounce either allows or impedes the air flow.)
5. Vowel exercises. *(*Massage jaw and let the air do the work from within.*)*
6. Agility.
7. Nya-nya-nya or other snarl exercises.
8. "Stretch the vowel open" as you go for higher notes.
9. Value of being VISUAL—if it looks good, it can be; if it looks tight or odd, it probably is.
10. Value of listening VERY carefully.
11. Value of regular review in books like Oren Brown and Lamperti.
12. Value of more physiological approach with certain people.
13. Importance of having a good coach/accompanist.
14. Importance of attitude.
15. Importance of *right* repertoire.

McDonald Studio Expectations

Fall 2002

1. **THE FIVE Ps: Proper Practice Prevents Poor Performance.** The important word here is "proper." Before you enter the practice room, know WHAT you wish to accomplish and HOW you can accomplish it. And remember that part of practice is drill, drill, drill—of the right things!!!
2. I expect each singer to keep a lesson notebook/ practice journal, which will be brought to each lesson and which will be used during/after each practice session to record exercises practiced and practice success/observations.
3. Before you begin singing a new piece, you should learn your text by speaking it until you no longer have to tell your mouth what to do; then speak it in the rhythm of the song. During the same period of time be learning the melody and rhythm by singing on a favorable vowel. After having done this preparation you will be ready to actually begin singing the piece. This may seem pedantic, but I guarantee that in 100% of cases, it will save time and ensure a piece better learned with fewer problems to "fix."
4. I will expect you to attend either the complete recital or the complete dress rehearsal of all recitalists in this studio. I will also expect you to attend either a final dress rehearsal or performance of all of the operas.

5. If you must miss a lesson for any reason, please let me know by the day before your lesson; otherwise I will not feel obligated to make up the lesson. Please do not come to lessons with a contagious disease. The only contagious state allowed is enthusiasm!

6. Buy a good small recorder which you can use during your practice sessions for immediate feedback and during your lessons. This can be very important since you are your own teacher six days a week.

7. A POSITIVE, ENTHUSIASTIC ATTITUDE, ADEQUATE REST, AND GOOD FOOD will help keep you healthy and on track! Note that ATTITUDE is first on this list!

8. The required book for the spring semester is *Caruso's Method of Tone Production* by Marafioti. Buy it now! We will refer to the book during lessons and Performance Classes.

9. Rules regarding performance requests: Clear ALL performance opportunities with me before you accept them. This includes solo performances within the school as well as outside its walls. Bring this repertoire to your lessons AT LEAST one month prior to the performance.

10. If you have questions about anything, please do not hesitate to ask me. This is your future you are building. I am delighted to be a part of your lives for a short time and to guide and help you achieve your goals and dreams.

Musings: MAY 2008

As human beings, our job in life is to help people realize how rare and valuable each one of us really is, that each of us has something that no one else has—or ever will have—something inside that is unique to all time. It's our job to encourage each other to discover that uniqueness and to provide ways of developing its expression.

Do what you think is right and let happen
what happens.
You may lose often—but that's not as
important.
What's important is living
according to principles.

Vision is a primary motivation
of human action.
It gives us the capacity
to live out of our imagination
instead of our memory.

Jim and former student Gordon Hawkins singing the *La Bohème* fourth act duet of Marcello and Rodolfo.

This was in our home in Loveland, Colorado, May 2010. Gordon had come to visit with Jim. They both sounded wonderful! Such joy!

TEACHING AT MIDDLEBURY
(1999-2010)

For twelve summers we taught in the Middlebury College Language Immersion Program in Middlebury, Vermont. Jim was Director of the *German for Singers and Vocal Coaches* portion of the German School and the resident voice instructor, and I was the students' vocal coach. Middlebury is nestled between the Green Mountains and the Alleghenies. On the weekends we so enjoyed exploring the bucolic countryside and its welcoming villages. Those twelve summers were special times for us as we worked *auf Deutsch* with our wonderful students and reveled in Vermont's beauty.

Jim with students from one of our *German for Singers and Vocal coaches* sessions, after the final concert of the summer.

Jim and his students at Indiana University.

THE NUGGETS

About the NUGGETS

Over his many years of teaching, Jim often referred to his thoughts, his musings about the voice, as "nuggets." He was a life-long student, reading all sorts of vocal pedagogy books. Undoubtedly the "nuggets" are a reflection of this study—his understanding of thoughts of others filtered through his own insights and experience, portraying his dedication to beautiful, holistic, healthful singing. Here are some examples of "nuggets":

How we pronounce either allows or impedes the air flow.

Technique is not something you superimpose on your voice; it's a systematic approach to the primal use of your body and voice.

Attitude plus imagination equals inspiration!

Cool head, warm heart.

One skill at a time.

Jim's teaching "bible," *Vocal Wisdom*, is a very well-worn book of insights into singing from a great teacher, Giovanni Battista Lamperti. One of Lamperti's students, William Earl Brown, compiled that collection. The format is simple—topical chapters with groups of a few thought-provoking lines at a time. Jim was indebted to Lamperti, using this little book in his teaching and his own vocal study, beginning in his undergraduate college days.

Lamperti: ***The foundation of all vocal study lies in the control of the breath.***

I've gathered the nuggets into categories of vocal topics, in no specific order within each category. Perhaps even one nugget's message might be mulled over for several days, or even weeks. It takes a long time to build a voice, a particularly challenging endeavor since one can't see or touch the instrument, or hear it as others do. So much of vocal success hinges upon the inclination and ability to believe in the power of one's imagination, and to trust that power.

I hope these thoughts are helpful to you, the reader, in this most worthy pursuit.

What is the golden rule of singing?

Know the result before you act.

NUGGETS ... IN GENERAL

Nugget*—a small lump of gold or other precious metal found ready-formed in the earth: a small chunk or lump of another substance.*

In General*—one uses "in general" to indicate speaking about something as a whole, rather than a part of it.*

It's interesting to think about Jim's use of the term *nugget* when referring to the individual notations found here and there in his collection of papers, or used as the title of his typed lists of thoughts for upcoming teaching. It seems to me that this myriad of seemingly random thoughts unite to form a basic compendium of his beliefs, strongly held and wisely implemented.

GENERAL NUGGETS

1. Develop a trust in what your mind and body can do.
2. Give a gift to your audience. You have something to say.
3. If it feels free when you sing, you know it is supported.
4. If it feels better, it sounds better.
5. If different feels better, it *is* better.
6. All change is not necessarily good—what is good change? Whatever makes singing easier, freer.
7. Have purposeful movement—gestures have to mean something dramatically.
8. Convince the audience of SOMETHING.
9. Always give 100% commitment, 150% smart, but rarely, maybe once in an opera, give 100% power.
10. Trying too hard can get you into trouble. Remember a Golden Rule of Singing (Lamperti): Know what you want to do—then DO it! That's it!
11. Respond to what you want without thinking or over-analyzing. Have a picture in your mind and make it come to life.

12. If you read something or someone tells you something that helps and doesn't harm your singing, then by all means use it.
13. People with good voices can make sounds that 'sound good,' but aren't optimal physically. Take responsibility for yourself.
14. Don't complicate the act of singing. You are just doing what you know how to do instinctively.
15. Try not to sound older or younger than you are, or create or manufacture sound. Sing with the natural, primal voice God gave you.
16. Approach everything from the positive.
17. Avoid listening to yourself too much. Be in the moment. Get out of yourself so you can get into your character.
18. Sing freely, as if you have no throat.
19. Good singing is simple. Aim for simplicity.
20. In an audition setting, even if you feel tentative, don't look it—make a good first impression.
21. Make sure your interpretive personality follows your train of thought.
22. Movement that doesn't have textual or musical meaning can be confusing to the audience.
23. Concentration is a calm feeling—like the Zen master.

24. Working smart is the key, not working "hard."

25. Why can't easy be right? It CAN BE ... and it IS.

26. "Sigh" into your tone.

27. You don't have to prove anything. Just sing!

28. When "supporting" your sound—use more air and less muscle. You don't have to FEEL the support for it to be there.

29. Let resonance and energy do the work for you.

30. Every voice has a speed it wants to move at, and tempo (within reason) should be decided accordingly.

31. Suspended notes suspend the audience's emotion. Give these their full due.

32. Be an active singer—you are constantly releasing tone, not clenching it. When the voice is "there," you aren't "putting" it there.

33. If we trust ourselves, we don't have to prove anything to anyone. We are not performing for approval.

TECHNIQUE

Technique—*a skillful or efficient way of doing or achieving something.*

Having accompanied Jim's voice lessons from our college undergraduate days through his master's and doctoral degrees, and listened to him practice in our small one-room apartment during his three years of study at the Hochschule für Musik in Munich, Germany, I am well aware of the many challenges one faces while developing a solid and workable singing technique.

Aspiring singers may be gifted with voices of great natural beauty; but to enjoy long-lived singing careers requires the nurturing and refinement of the total instrument—body, mind, spirit, and voice. Furthermore, the mastery once achieved must be constantly refined as the voice and body mature and change. The quest is a noble and challenging one.

TECHNIQUE NUGGETS

One skill at a time.

1. Technique is not something you superimpose on your voice; it's a systematic approach to the primal use of your body and your voice.
2. Primal is very energetic, but it's not fighting yourself. It's let-go-ness, so that you never feel like you are pushing sound—you are always "drawing the thread."
3. Primal sounds are sounds that respond to a primal emotion, joy (laughter), fear, surprise, hurt, disappointment (groan). But they are not emotions that are manufactured in some "acting" process. They are original sounds, primal sounds—unlearned.
4. The voice "adjusts," but you don't "adjust" it; it just happens!
5. There is no one "answer" to singing well—except for the answer, "coordination." But to achieve the right coordination takes years of proper practice of the right elements, and the putting together of those elements into "coordination."
6. Those who tend to sing too loudly get the voice too thick on the staff and then the top is either not there or is pushed.
7. Keep nose in the tone, but not the tone in the nose.

8. Don't breathe with your eyebrows or shoulders.
9. When singing, the spine should stay unswayed.
10. Never dig into notes—spring off from them.
11. Technical ease is for the purpose of delight in words and music.
12. Whispering and clearing the throat puts unnatural strain on the cords. A less abusive way is to hum for 30 seconds, and to drink water.
13. The tongue is released forward for high notes—it should not tense up or wiggle around. Imagine eating an ice cream cone or placing a lemon drop on your tongue.
14. When you lick an ice cream cone, you automatically breathe—it is the beginning of a yawn kind of feeling.
15. Sirens are cultivated, educated screams.
16. Visualize the ends of tones releasing comfortably and the voice will respond to that. Don't stop or start the tone with the throat. If the throat is right, the tone is right.
17. The voice is always above the roof of the mouth.
18. The tone starts from ease, not from effort.
19. If your coloratura gets 'stuck,' your throat is trying to get involved. Just dance to the tempo

of your inner conductor—respond and the throat will move out of the way.

20. To the hearer, the voice must sound even; to the singer, it will feel and sound different in different parts of the range.
21. No note should feel like it's your highest, even if it is!
22. Passaggio approach: a bridge across a chasm has to be able to connect on both sides. Many people will try to build the passaggio from below, causing push.
23. If the middle is too fat, thick, big, loud, the top will be difficult at best. Sing with the right "mix" and you won't have this problem.
24. Singing softly is not giving less of something—it is merely giving more of something else.
25. "Cover" simply means the tone is covered with overtones,—not manufacturing an artificial cover by pressing with the back of the tongue. "Cover" is the result of the right deep throat.
26. Excessive upper body strength is not necessary—not even desirable. But the tone of the body is very important.
27. The soprano "sitz" is a vocal position. It is above the roof of the mouth, in the middle of the forehead. Feel and observe the resonance ..

in these places, not in the mouth. When this is right it should have spin.

28. When you are singing in the middle range (on the staff), which are the notes in the "sitz", the higher notes will exist properly. Observe this "sitz." Don't create it; otherwise, you run the risk of pinching in the throat. The chest voice exists similarly, as long as it is "in the sitz."

29. Your voice can be as round and as rich as it wants to be in the sitz range, as long as it is in the sitz. Don't try to create anything outside of the sitz.

30. The ability of the chest (rib cage) and back to "resist" without making the diaphragm and epigastrium rigid is vital.

31. "Sigh" into your tone. When "supporting" your sound, use more air and less muscle. You don't have to feel the support for it to be there.

32. Be an active singer—you are constantly releasing tone, not clenching it. When the voice is "there," you aren't "putting" it there.

33. The middle of the road is a great place to stay. Know when you need athleticism; know when you need limpidity.

34. The music of the poetry can be practiced—and can indeed help—at the same time technique is being worked on.

35. If we let the words lead us, we will be convincing performers.

-36. Longer notes can't be "held." They are sustained with breath energy.

37. Short notes have long sounds.

38. When we "think" the pitch, the throat is automatically ready to produce that pitch.

39. As Pavarotti said: "Singing is imitating a baby screaming in the cradle."

40. Support is like a dance of the breath inside the scaffolding of the body.

41. When "supporting" your sound, use more air and less muscle.

42. Release tones without the use of your throat, always.

43. You cannot sing well until your least "hum" excites your whole co-ordination as much as your loudest tone.

44. You cannot sing with your mouth open if you cannot do so with it shut.

45. Let the voice show who *you* are. It will come forward if you let it. If you try to make it do this or that, it can never be free to show you what it can do, or who you are.

46. Sing from the crotch.

REPERTOIRE CHOICES

During his years of teaching, Jim accrued a sizeable library of vocal music and scores. He would spend many hours perusing this library to find just the right repertoire for his students, matching their vocal maturity, language and technical challenges with songs and arias that would meet and stretch their capabilities. Here are his thoughts about such decision-making:

"Everyone has strengths and weaknesses. We should, in general, choose repertoire that displays our strengths and disguises our weaknesses. The correct repertoire choices can make a huge difference in how one appears to those listening, and in how one feels about oneself.

Things to take into account when making repertoire choices include a whole range of considerations, but certainly include:

Range **Fach**

Tessitura **Language**

Tempo **Phrase Length**

Coloratura demands

Sostenuto demands

Amount of text to be learned

Aspects to balance other repertoire

Opinions of teachers and coaches."

MUSICIANSHIP

As Heinrich Heine wrote: "What is music? ... the very existence of music is wonderful, I might even say miraculous. Its domain is between thought and phenomena. ... it hovers between spirit and matter, related to both, yet differing from each. It is spirit, but it is spirit subject to the measurement of time. It is matter, but it is matter that can dispense with space."

Musicianship—*knowledge, skill and artistic sensitivity in performing music.*

What is musicianship? Are aspects of it learned or inborn? Listing its specific characteristics becomes an almost impossible task. It is something we as listeners recognize, appreciate, and value; but it is difficult to define its many intangible components.

A performer's keen musicianship is what allows music to be "miraculous," as Heine said—to be all it can be for the performer, and for the listener. To acquire the knowledge, skill and artistic sensitivity needed for affecting music-making requires years of awareness and devoted effort. Following are some of Jim's nuggets about aspects of musicianship, that elusive essence of beautiful music-making.

MUSICIANSHIP NUGGETS

Cool head, warm heart.

1. If you are aware of what you want in terms of interpretation, it will come. It's those who really think and prepare mentally who are individualistic as performers.
2. Be aware of the harmonic color of the music itself and let the thoughts and voice change when it changes.
3. When performing is predictable, the listener can simply switch off. If we want to be interesting, we have to find ways of being imaginative and unpredictable.
4. In learning texts of Art Song, practice singing with just the left hand piano part to place the text on the rhythm of the song.
5. One hallmark of a true artist is an excitement that is maintained in the least demanding places of the composition.
6. Expression doesn't come solely from the face, but also from the body and the voice.
7. When you repeat a phrase, make it different each time.
8. A deaf person and a blind person should know what you are singing about.

9. Keep your focus during musical interludes—remember subtext.

10. Suspended notes suspend the audience's emotions. Give these their full due.

11. It matters not whether your voice be phenomenal or even beautiful; if it expresses the music and the words, you will have an interested audience.

2. When wanting to sing softly, sing with the intention of being soft, not off the voice.

13. Rallentando in Monteverdi happens in the middle of the phrase. If one does it at every cadence, there will be no flow to the music.

14. In Monteverdi, all recitative is in 4 or in 2. The secret to pacing is thinking 4 or 2 as necessary.

    2 = solemnity, coldness.

    4 = agitation.

15. When the text wants to go on, go on. Especially at cadences note values are flexible.

16. Know exactly what you are singing about so you can be engaging to your audience.

17. Invent the future out of imagination rather than be limited by the past.

PRACTICE

One skill at a time

Practice—*repeated performance or systematic exercise for acquiring skill or proficiency.*

Truth be told, in my awareness it took Jim a long time to develop a workable and reliable approach to vocal practice. It took him a long time to recognize the importance of a disciplined regimen necessary for developing the right musculature balances needed for good vocal growth. He had some early unhelpful habits to correct, and this process was one of great and intense frustration to him. I think he also had to learn that intellect alone will not fix an ingrained habit. I believe that this arduous journey of discovery and development contributed much to his effectiveness as a teacher.

PRACTICE ROUTINE

1. **Warm up**: Warm up until you feel that your voice is responding/doing what you want it to do.

2. **Vocalize:** Sing vocal exercises with specific goals in mind but don't get uptight. Simply sing!

3. **Repertoire:** Get it in the voice. Apply these steps every day, throughout all of your practice.

PRACTICE NUGGETS

1. When practicing, know what you want to accomplish before you go into the practice room.
2. The body can only do what the brain is thinking.
3. If you aren't getting the results you want doing something the same way over and over, try different approaches. Even do the exact opposite of what you intend, to bring yourself back to the middle of the road.
4. When practicing, practice at the optimum time of day for you—not after you have done everything else!
5. Practice just until you get tired—this is how you build muscles.
6. Remember what you learn, then put it into practice. Remember and do.

RECORD YOUR PRACTICE

RESONANCE

Resonance—*amplification of the range of audibility of any source of speech sounds, especially of phonation, by various couplings of the cavities of the mouth, nose, sinuses, and the skeletal structure of the head and upper chest.*

There was a time in Jim's vocal development that his voice sounded better to me when he was singing Italian than it did in German or English. Then that changed. Why did it change? I can only surmise that once he realized the importance of the Italian freedom and release of the jaw and tongue, all of his singing had beautiful resonance.

RESONANCE NUGGETS

1. We want to develop resonance, not loudness.
2. Let resonance and energy do the work for you.
3. Some kind of resonance is always prepared when you take your breath. What do you prepare?
4. The resonance (float of the voice) comes to join the breath compression rather than pushing the breath at the resonance. (One analogy is the balance of the fishing float, the line, and the weight by the hook.)
5. Let the resonance simply flop around in your head. Never try to make a lot of sound—just trust your resonance: let resonance and energy do the work for you.

DICTION

Diction—*the style of enunciation in speaking or singing.*

A hallmark of Jim's singing was his clear, understandable diction. Was it clear because he was devoted to the beauty of poetic texts? I don't know the answer as we never spoke about his diction during his performing career. There was no need. I always found great joy in playing for him, as his excellent diction coupled with his innate musicality brought clarity to the shape of musical phrases and thus to the music's emotional impact. Great credit is due those who in any language or genre make the effort needed to cherish texts and work carefully to sing them clearly, knowing that words and music enhance and support each other.

DICTION NUGGETS—Italian Diction Style

1. Legato—practically no consonants at all, especially m" and "n."
2. In Romance languages, stress is done *not* by emphasizing consonants, but rather by lengthening vowels.
3. Open up all final vowels (libiamo). Doing this takes more energy because the sound is continuous, rather than shorter.
4. Above the staff, no consonants. No plosives ever.
5. A loose jaw is necessary. Consonants must not "freeze" the jaw. In correct Italian, there is no "mouthiness."

1. **GOOD DICTION IS**:
   Correct—"native" sounding
   Clear—with understandable vowels and consonants
   Free—articulators are to articulate, not to do double duty by energizing or supporting the sound.

2. Diction is simply a series of sounds, which can be done either freely or conversely, sadly, with tight articulators and instrument.

3. "Inner Diction" is proper, free cooperation of the palate, unhinged jaw and released tongue.

4. IPA (International Phonetic Alphabet)—a very useful tool. It has limitations as it cannot accurately reproduce all the subtleties of any language. But it does a wonderful job of getting one in the "ballpark."

5. German "schwa" (the unaccented "e") is a variable sound colored by the preceding main vowel.

6. Consonants—articulated in many cases with the tip of the tongue, like in the Italian language.

7. Consonant exercises—how we pronounce either allows or impedes the flow of air (as in ... Butterfly-touch consonants, sneeze consonants).

8. Glottals can be like an Italian saying "ah, cara!" They can function with a "slap" together of the cords, or start from closed cords which simply separate to make a gentle glottal. Your choice. They do not have to be vocally unhealthy.
9. You don't have to resort to overuse of the lips, mouth and jaw to be understood. Practice "inner diction." (i.e. letting the released tongue do the articulation, as in Italian diction)
10. Proper pronunciation of all vowels and consonants relieves back of tongue tension.
11. Vowel exercises: massage jaw and let the air do the work from within.
12. Vowel modification is important to the success of various parts of the voice.
13. Think the French nasal [oe] on top for the right resonance/vowel.

NUGGETS

from study with SIR PETER PEARS

P.P.—"*Credo in Rubato*"

P.P.—"*Ben (*Benjamin Britten*) was one of those pianists who could make the piano sound uncommonly like the harpsichord. The sort of 'dryness' that he liked came to his fingers easily.*"

P.P.—B.B. was a master of the half-pedal.

P.P.—B.B. was very conscious of the rhythmical possibilities in Purcell's recitatives (which have the feeling of arioso).

McD—P.P. naturally revels in the color and expressive qualities inherit in words and musical phrases.

P.P.—In *On This Island,* Britten tried to get away from what he had been taught at the Royal College—influenced by John Ireland, etc., who were under the influence of German and French art song's syllabic text settings. Britten broke away from that in these songs. He opened the door and let air in. He knew Purcell and Schubert hadn't followed that maxim of one note per syllable.

P.P.—Purcell was a man of the theater. We must remember that when performing his music. In "Music for Awhile," Britten's realization of Purcell's music kept Purcell's brilliance, strangeness, color, and character, but was very personal at the same time. This was different from more academic styles of realizations/settings.

P.P.—Purcell's recitatives must have the feeling of a tempo or they fall to pieces.

P.P.—Using portamento is one of the best ways to practice because it keeps everything on the same line.

P.P.—In Bach arias, where words are repeated over and over again, after a bit it's more important to sing the music than the words.

P.P.—Let the voice sing itself, especially on long runs. Don't manufacture it.

P.P.—In phrasing (particularly in 3/8 and 6/8) you <u>never</u> have equal weight on all notes. The second is nearly always lighter.

P.P.—*"I don't want to try to sing every note beautifully, but rather interestingly, or colorfully."*

P.P.—Technique must function as a liberator of the imagination in the service of the composer.

P.P.—An awful lot of singing is effort of will—you make up your mind and *do it.* It's not enough to make up your mind.

ADDENDUM

BIOGRAPHIES

Jim and Annie

JAMES RAY "Jim" MCDONALD received his M.M. and D.M.A. degrees from the University of Iowa, where he studied with Herald I. Stark. After three years in Munich, Germany, on Fulbright and German Academic Exchange Service grants, he began his 43 years of teaching voice. He first taught at Ohio Wesleyan University, then at Millikin University, followed by the University of Maryland for nineteen years where he was chair of the Voice/Opera Department for eleven years and helped create the Maryland Opera Studio.

He taught at Indiana University from 1995-2005, at New England Conservatory of Music until 2008, and in retirement at Colorado State University. His many performances included the International Handel Festival in Halle, East Germany; Aldeburgh, England; the Library of Congress; the National Symphony Orchestra; and at Kennedy Center as a member of Theater Chamber Players, Kennedy Center's resident chamber music ensemble, directed by Dina Koston and Leon Fleisher.

For twelve summers he was Director of the *German for Singers and Vocal Coaches* portion of the Middlebury College summer language immersion program. He taught master classes at the Music Academy in Baku, Azerbaijan, served as a voice teacher at the Britten-Pears School for Advanced Musical Studies, was a master class teacher in the Princeton University Summer Program, and a Master Teacher for the National Association of Teachers of Singing Intern Program.

RUTH ANN "Annie" MCDONALD was an official pianist for the Belvedere International Vocal Competition, the Kennedy Center Rockefeller Competition, and the Marion Anderson International Vocal Competition. She coached singers at the American Institute of Musical Studies (AIMS) in Graz, Austria, and three opera premieres at the Kammeroper in Vienna, Austria.

For twelve summers she was the vocal coach on the faculty of Vermont's Middlebury College *German for Singers and Vocal Coaches* program. She coached students at University of Maryland, Catholic University of America, Indiana University, New England Conservatory, and Colorado State University.

Recital appearances include concerts with Sir Peter Pears, George Shirley, Phyllis Bryn-Julsen, Gordon Hawkins, Kammersängerin Julie Kaufmann, her late husband, Dr. James McDonald, and performances with the Theater Chamber Players of Kennedy Center.

Her other four-decades-long, much-loved career was as a church musician in liturgical churches, where she was Director of Music, serving as organist and director of adult and children's choirs. Her bachelor and master's degrees are in Organ Performance and her doctorate is in Vocal Coaching and Piano Accompaniment.

In an Email to his students at New England Conservatory, 10/28/2008, Jim wrote ...

"To everyone,

I came across this email which Annie had sent to a student in the past. Since I know that all of us deal with these issues from time to time, and since I think this email is so good, I wanted to share it with all of you. If it helps anyone now, or in the future, then it's done its job once again!

Best, McD"

Hi! I can understand your having a crisis of confidence. You're getting feedback that may appear to you to be somewhat critical of your performing, and of your singing. What's really happening is that people believe in your talent and they/we are pushing your envelope, trying to move you beyond where you are—into a newer and hopefully better place. This can be very difficult for young musicians. It's difficult for old musicians, too. :-) But it's really an important part of our development as artists. I have two thoughts for you:

First: performers need to have a "tough skin" because we are never free from criticism and new ideas may be disconcerting.

Second: and this is, to my mind, incredibly important—we must have trust. Have you ever thought about how much having trust plays a role in our lives? We have trust when we eat in a restaurant that the food will be healthful. We have trust that the products we buy and use every day will be safe and effective. That our bed won't collapse while we sleep. That our roof will keep the rain out. That morning will come. That spring will be sprung. And on and on. Why then is it so difficult for us to trust ourselves and our gifts? I urge you to try to do that ... to trust the very hard work you do. To trust your voice will respond. To trust your ability to be expressive. To trust that your audience will enjoy what you share with them. To trust the integrity of the gift you've been given.

If we do *our* share, which you certainly are doing by being a conscientious student, then we can let go and trust that our gift will do *its* share. Worrying and feeling unconfident are negative energies. Please try to let go of those and instead fill every pore of your being with confident trust. I think you'll be thrilled with how helpful that can be for you. And when you do get feedback that threatens your self-confidence, just know that perhaps that feedback will be helpful to you the next time you sing. Remember, we are all "works in progress."

With love, Mrs. McD

It's through opening the Inner Life ...

that one opens the voice.

Annie

POSTSCRIPT

This brief retrospective of Jim's life and teaching would only be complete with mention of his artistic gifts and his sense of humor. He created distinctive assemblages out of found wood and did beautiful wooden carvings, especially of birds, our dog "Four Sox," cats, and dancers. He loved to pun, which he did with alacrity in both English and German, and he particularly reveled in the art of the limerick. He even wrote series of them as tributes for friends' birthdays. It was remarkable how quick was his wit, evoking wonderful laughter from his friends, with sparkle in his kindly blue eyes famously crowned by his amazingly bushy eyebrows!

LETTERS from WILLIAM S. BRADY (1878-1957) to HERALD I. STARK (1907-1997)

March 9, 1936: When you take your breath, please remember that three-fifths of the lungs are in the back of the body, and that the lower lobes especially can be sensed only by the expansion of the back. The lungs have five lobes, the right lung three, the left one two. These lobes do not connect with each other, they connect only with the central passage way, the trachea. Do not forget that every vowel is echoed in the abdomen and that in singing the lower lobes lose their breath in order to make the tone-part of the chest constantly expand.

November 16, 1936: Practice carefully with breathing exercises. Inflate the nostrils, close the lips gently with the idea that the lips are free and loosened from the teeth and gums. This is very important. Do your humming exercises, seeing to it that the chest remains pneumatic, never going down, and that the abdominal pressure becomes stronger and more supple with use. Do not forget that the line of the voice is felt from the bridge of the nose, down to the diaphragmatic pressure, and that the peak of the soft palate must be examined, that the tongue rests against the lower teeth and that the larynx must be supple, but strong, connecting with the sternum, but there is a decided pressure of the vowel against the sternum and larynx.

Pronounce your exercises three or four times before you sing them. Be careful to begin extended exercises from above the upper tone. Watch constantly the feeling of your larynx, sternum and tongue while doing this. Do not forget that high notes are attacked from above the back of the head, which serves to elevate the peak of the palate. Never allow yourself to force, and do not practice when too tired physically.

Above all, remember to speak your phrases first several times and to sing them, trying to capture their spoken position. You will find after a while that taking the breath through the dilated nostrils with loosened lips meeting will give you a very visible idea of larynx, tongue and sternum, with the peak of the palate at one end of your position and the diaphragm at the other end.

November 14, 1939: Please take your breath slowly and deeply as always through the inflated nostrils. Watch the position of the palate, never changing it. You will find the voice going over the palate to the nose and to the masque without your will. Never try to place it over. Speak deep and always feel when you sing that your breath is coming in. Constantly keep the sensation of breath coming in. Do not try to place the voice high over the roof of the mouth against the nose. That will take care of itself.

William S. Brady graduated from Cincinnati College of Music in 1900 and did advanced study in Germany and Italy. He was a successful and venerated teacher in New York City, also doing master classes in Chicago and Munich, Germany.

Comments from Students

It is always a treat to hear from former students and to learn what paths their lives have taken. One of our students from the days at Indiana University was a young man from Missouri, Josh Whitener. In one of our emails back and forth, he mentioned how meaningful he found Jim's comparison of head resonance to a coal miner's head lamp. What?? At that point in our teaching lives, I was rarely in Jim's lessons, so I had never heard that analogy. Josh kindly agreed to write down his thoughts about some of the concepts he learned during his study with my husband.

"Dr. J" and Josh Whitener, after Josh's Junior Recital, Indiana University, May 2003

***Josh Whitener* writes:** *While there are many things I learned from Dr. J (*with Jim's consent, this is the moniker used by his students at Indiana University*) here are some of the things that have had the strongest impact on my singing and teaching. For example:*

1. Die Aussprache ist eine Reihenfolge von Geräuschen—Diction is a sequence of sounds:

Dr. J brought this concept to my attention during my time at the Middlebury College German for Singers Program – hence the German description. This is wonderful approach for developing clear diction in singing. He and Annie both wanted me to master all language sounds first individually and then to practice combining them into a sequence of sounds. This was opposed to immediately trying to sing the text of songs – something that the majority of young singers do.

I was initially to practice any difficult or new sounds slowly and out of context. For example, in discovering the correct sound of a mixed vowel such as [y], I was to break down the process mechanically, first saying [i] followed by the lip rounding of an [u]. After all problematic speech sounds were mastered, I was to then recite all of the song's speech sounds in a sigh-like monotone manner (without pitches or rhythm) connecting them into a sequence (Reihenfolge). Attention was to be paid to a free and natural movement of the articulatory muscles and jaw. The next step was to recite the text in the rhythm of the song or aria, which was continued in this sigh-like manner. This all led to the final step of singing the text with the correct rhythm and pitches.

This whole process was to be done slowly over a couple of days in short intensive sessions. In fact, Dr. J recommended practice throughout the entire day instead of at one particular sitting, so as to continually reinforce good habits. The singer was not to rush the process. Their point was that good diction was the result of a physiological process, rather than an intellectual one. Thus, by slowing down and breaking up the diction into these various simple steps, the articulatory muscles would learn to respond automatically, resulting in clear sung diction. This process does wonders for any sung text regardless of the language.

2. ***Coal miner lamps:*** The sympathetic resonance changes—which a singer feels in the head throughout the various registers—are a valuable tool the singer has in creating an "even" voice, without sudden register shifts. Dr. J was resolute from day one that one should never place a tone; but he did want the singer to be aware of the changes he or she felt while singing throughout his or her vocal range. One particular image unique to Dr. J's teaching was imagery he used of a coal miner wearing two lamps on his head - one at his forehead (between the eyebrows) and one at crown of the head. Dr. J stated that for sung notes in the lower range (middle voice), the lamp at the forehead would be the brightest. As one ascended the scale, the other lamp (at the crown of the head) would gradually light up, and for the highest tones of a singer's vocal range, the lamp at the crown of the head would be the brightest.

He consistently stressed that both lamps should never completely go dark. For example, while the singer's lowest sung notes would create more sympathetic resonance sensations at the forehead (i.e. a brighter light at the lamp at the forehead), the singer was always to remember that the light at the crown of the head would not go completely dark; thus, the singer should continue to maintain a feeling of backspace. The same was true about the notes in the highest range: Here the lamp at the crown of the head would be brighter, but the singer was not to forget the lamp at the forehead.

3. ***Let your body teach you how to sing – The Primal Approach:***

An essential point Dr. J reinforced was the belief that my body could teach me to sing better than I could in my attempts to "control" my voice. He strongly believed a singer needed to tap into his or her natural ability and trust this primal nature. In fact, he often stressed that the primal nature was the best teacher.

Often at the start of my lessons, he asked me to not sing but rather just make "primal sounds" (sounds like a cry, laugh or a sigh); or to notice how my breathing functioned naturally when I "wasn't trying;" or to simply notice where I felt sympathetic resonance sensations rather than "making" them happen. This approach serves as a wonderful starting point for any singer, and has helped me greatly to stay on track. As Dr. J. would expect and hope for, I incorporate this approach into my daily warm up, and I am "passing it forward," teaching these techniques to my voice students.

Tenor **Josh Whitener** *is engaged at the National Theater Mannheim, Germany. His many guest appearances include Teatro alla Scala and the Salzburg Festival. He specializes in the Mozart and bel canto tenor roles, the German romantic repertoire, and concert performances of Bach, Beethoven and Verdi. His doctorate in voice is from Indiana University Jacobs School of Music where he taught as an Associate Instructor of Voice. He has taught at Julius-Maximilians-Universität Würzburg and maintains a private voice studio.*

Mark Whitmire, *received his Doctorate of Musical Arts degree from the University of Maryland. He has been Adjunct Professor of Music and Liturgy at Virginia Theological Seminary and Professor of Music at Northern Virginia Community College for 33 years, He is also Director of Music for St. James Episcopal Church in Richmond, Virginia, where his wife Virginia is organist.*

***Mark Whitmire* writes:**

I was privileged to study singing with Dr. James McDonald at the University of Maryland from Fall 1983 until I finished my doctoral coursework in Fall 1986. Dr. McDonald continued to guide me through the dissertation process until completion in 1991. Without his wisdom and encouragement, I am certain that I could never have completed the degree.

Dr. McDonald's pedagogical approach was not unfamiliar to me when I came to UMCP. My previous teacher, Prof. Herald Stark, had been his teacher at the University of Iowa. Both Dr. McDonald and Prof. Stark spoke often of the pedagogical approach of William S. Brady (1878-1957), a founding member The American Academy of Teachers of Singing, who had been Prof. Stark's teacher in New York City. I was privileged to have a connection to an important pedagogical lineage.

As a voice teacher, the most important lesson I learned from Dr. McDonald is to listen. While this seems obvious, it is not always the case with singing teachers. Many subscribe to a "method" and the tenets of that method are taught to every singer in the studio. Dr. McDonald realized that the vocal technique needs of each singer are different, and he used his ear to craft an individual plan to address those needs. He was equally skilled in assessing the unique personality of each student and adapted his approach accordingly.

As a singer, the most important lesson I learned from Dr. McDonald is to fully understand and engage with text. My area of concentration was 20th-century English song, and Dr. McDonald was a noted authority on this topic. He passed along to me his love of the music of Benjamin Britten. Britten's selection of texts and their treatment became my dissertation topic. Under Dr. McDonald's guidance I learned close reading of poetry and how to internalize the text. I learned that each text presents a range of possible interpretations and that it was essential to make the words your own.

Finally, and perhaps most importantly, I learned from Dr. McDonald's manner of interacting with students. He brought into the studio a sense of humanity. He saw us all not only as his students, but as complete human beings, with families and complex lives in which music plays a very important part.

Mark Whitmire writes about his work with Eric Crozier:

One of the many gifts I received from Dr. McDonald was an introduction to Eric Crozier and Nancy Evans. When Eric and Nancy travelled to the US to visit the McDonalds, I was given the honor of picking them up at Dulles airport. Eric never failed to thank me for coming out on that cold, rainy wintry night. During the week of their residence at Maryland, I sang Mozart, Dowland, Purcell, and Britten for them. They shared keen insights into interpretation and vocal technique and suggested I apply for admission to the Britten-Pears School. In the summer of 1985 I attended the English Song Course there, where I took lessons with Sir Peter Pears—a life-changing experience. In addition, I had coaching sessions with Theodore Uppman (the original *Billy Budd*), and Nancy Evans. I also enjoyed sessions with Eric, who generously shared his immense knowledge of literature and his keen interest in the poetry of Thomas Hardy.

Eric suggested I might write my doctoral dissertation on Britten's song cycle *Winter Words,* set to Hardy's poetry; and he offered to assist me and serve on my dissertation committee. The hours I spent in the Britten-Pears Library looking at each annotated page of Britten's own copy of Hardy's poems and at the original manuscript of *Winter Words* were the beginning of the long process of writing the paper entitled "*Songs by John Ireland and Benjamin Britten to Texts by Thomas Hardy.*" Eric gave me keen insights and well-placed criticisms along the way. I owe my deepest thanks to Eric Crozier for his generosity of spirit, and to Dr. James McDonald—teacher, mentor, and friend.

Benjamin Czarnota *is a unique pedagogue who seeks to address singers' individual needs and facilitate growth as an artist, each with their own distinct voice. He is a performer, teacher, coach, composer, and arranger with degrees in both music theory and voice performance, solid piano skills, and experience in musical styles ranging from blues to rock to opera, After 15 years teaching at the undergraduate level, while maintaining a private studio, he has returned to the Jacobs School of Music at Indiana University to complete his doctorate in Music Literature and Performance with a Graduate Certificate in Vocology (anticipated 2023).*

***Benjamin Czarnota* writes:**

A truly pivotal moment in my singing was, ironically, when Dr. James McDonald told me to "stop singing." I was a year into my graduate study at Indiana University and was having trouble with a particular passage from *La Bohème*. I walked into my lesson, quite frustrated, and told him that I was at a complete loss. He calmy asked me to show him the page in the score in question. I did so and, somewhat mindlessly, "marked" my way through the bars—just so he could be reminded of the melodic line. He immediately remarked: "What was wrong with that?" With a hint of bewildered indignation, I responded that "I wasn't really singing." With a chuckle and a slight lift of his exceptional eyebrows, he exclaimed, "Well then—stop singing!"

What followed was one of the more meaningful voice lessons of my life. I learned the extent to which I had relied upon kinesthetic feedback and perceived effort in my approach to singing. Really "singing" (by my definition) meant applying a certain amount of breath pressure with consistency, with a corresponding engagement in my vocal tract that I could feel. My "marked" passage at the beginning of the lesson didn't have that sort of energized drive or feedback. It was, rather, somewhat tossed off. He assured me that my casual rendition when I wasn't "singing" was more than ample soundwise and, in fact, more resonant than my customary singing. Liberated from my focus on what I was "doing" in order to make what I thought was an ideal sound, I was left to attend to quite different things: language, intention, musical phrasing, and more. These were the elements that comprised real singing, by his definition.

The "ideal" sound was the one that arose, somewhat serendipitously, from the heart of an artist willing to trust that the technical foundation had already been laid.

In my own teaching for over a decade since that crucial lesson, I have tried to keep in the back of my mind the essential goal of guiding my students into a relationship with their voices that was more about discovering and marrying vocal sound to their individual human expression than it was about making any particular "right" sound. Singing is not mere noisemaking; it is the act of sharing the human experience through released, harnessed vocalized energy.

In my own singing, if I'm honest, I still struggle with wanting to be able to control and manufacture a particular sound from time to time. When I do, I try to remember Dr. McDonald's gentle exhortation to "stop singing," take a breath, and set about the business of being the most authentic artist I can be, trusting that what comes out will be better than anything I could have devised beforehand.

Gordon Hawkins *has been critically acclaimed throughout the world for his in-depth interpretations and luxuriant baritone voice. A winner of the Metropolitan Opera National Council Auditions and the George London Grant recipient, he has been praised for his rich lyricism as well as his dramatic instinct. He is a winner of the Luciano Pavarotti Competition and in 2006 was honored as the Washington National Opera "Artist of the Year."*

His engagements include Amonasro in Aida with Houston Grand Opera and Cincinnati Opera; a gala concert for the Supreme Court Justices in Washington, D.C.; the title role in Macbeth with Seattle Opera; Tonio in I Pagliacci with Atlanta Opera; Porgy in Porgy and Bess with Seattle Opera, Washington National Opera and Michigan Opera Theatre; High Priest in Samson et Dalila with Opera Ontario; Villains in Les Contes d'Hoffman in Tokyo, and Tonio/Alfio in Manitoba Opera's double bill of I Pagliacci/Cavalleria Rusticana. He starred in the world premiere of the new opera "Blue." Opera News wrote: "It was through his voice that we began to comprehend the depth of sorrow at the core of the work." Gordon Hawkins is Professor of Voice at Arizona State University.

***Gordon Hawkins* writes:**

When I was a student of Jim's at the University of Maryland, I was asked to perform Benjamin Britten's *Journey of the Magi* with Jim and Derek Lee Ragin for the Theater Chamber Players of Kennedy Center. Knowing that Jim and Derek would be so well prepared put a great deal of pressure on me. But after we began working on it, all of that pressure went away. It wasn't so much that we were singing but that we were expressing musical thoughts and ideas. I am trying to recall whether I was actually aware of this concept prior to that, and I appreciated how much freedom of imagination I was allowed to have.

My students come to me wanting to know how to do a certain thing without ever thinking about what role their imagination plays in singing. Once I can get them to free themselves from ego constraints of right and wrong and think about what it is they actually want to say, does real singing begin.

Susan Bender *is a versatile soprano who has been featured as a soloist with orchestras and opera companies across the country, including the Metropolitan Opera Orchestra as a National Council Winner. She was recruited to serve in the United States Navy Sea Chanter Chorus and is recorded on the Naxos and Albany labels. Her work on the stage includes Gilbert and Sullivan operettas with Interact Theater, garnering her two Helen Hayes nominations from the Washington Theater Awards Association. Other roles include Norina in Don Pasquale, Susanna in The Marriage of Figaro, Poussette in Massenet's Manon, Diana in Hippolyte et Aricie and Damigella in Monteverdi's L'incoronazione di Poppea.*

Professor Bender teaches voice and opera at the University of Wisconsin, Stevens Point. Her students have gone on to professional singing careers on Broadway and at the Metropolitan Opera, while current students continue to win awards at state and regional NATS competitions and placements in prestigious summer and graduate programs.

Susan Bender writes:

What I would love to add here is the humanity Jim showed his students. I try to remember this always when dealing with undergraduates; they are figuring out who they are and are often in need of a patient guiding hand. Jim would often say that 90% of voice teaching is psychological, and he didn't just mean finding imagery to discover the voice (the sculptor revealing the art by chipping away that which does not belong comes to mind here).

He also was intent upon students finding their bliss which, in turn, could and often did, unlock the voice within. He didn't only quote Lamperti! I remember him quoting Marjorie Bairstow, Eloise Ristad, Kahlil Gibran, among other writers in an effort to spark the imagination, to say something, to release sounds held within. This was how I found my voice with Jim not once, but often.

Rachel and "McD"
After a performance at
New England Conservatory
2008

Rachel Eve Holmes *is an American soprano recently described as "expressive and subtle, with a stunning instrument" (Capital Times). A Georgia native, her performing career has taken her to Belgium, China, Italy, Austria, Canada, and the Czech Republic. She is the winner of numerous vocal competitions. Her most recent performance was the much anticipated debut recital at Carnegie Hall's Weill Recital Hall.*

Dr. Holmes studied with James McDonald at New England Conservatory of Music and Colorado State University, and did her doctorate in voice at the University of Wisconsin. She is Director of Opera at Reinhardt University, Executive Director of Peach State Opera, and is represented by VAMS Artist Management.

***Rachel Eve Holmes* writes:**

I echo Dr. McDonald's philosophies in my work as a performer, director, and voice teacher, as they are guiding stars that direct my path every day in all that I do. When thinking back on the years we spent together from 2005-2011, a few things come to mind. I often used language with McD (as we affectionately called him at NEC) that he was "building my voice". He corrected me to say that all we were doing was releasing what was already inside, not building. He would say to me frequently, "It's all there—it's always been there. We just have to release all interference so it can emerge". This has helped me greatly, and the students whom I now teach as well. It was (and still is) about "allowing" more than "doing." Letting the voice emerge as it was naturally intended, instead of trying to lead the voice along, like a stubborn dog on a leash!

He frequently pointed to a quote on his studio door: "Know your limitations, and then surpass them." He helped me realize that often the only people who allow our own limitations are ourselves. With trust, belief, and allowing, our truest selves and voices can emerge, and therefore be of the most use to the world.

Dr. McDonald helped me expand my personality and find freedom in my expression. He was passionate about teaching us to teach ourselves, allowing our innate artistry to take over, so we could gain full agency over it. He was always direct and honest but tempered with humor and kindness. He was a leader who wanted all of us to become leaders through solving our own problems, by building our own knowledge and understanding of ourselves and our process as performers. Instead of imposing his will on us, he gave us ours, and helped us to trust it. He often encouraged me that I had something unique to say that no one else could say for me, and it was my responsibility to first reveal it, and then share it.

Whenever there was interference in my “flow phonation,” (the freedom in my sound), he would make a gesture of an X with his arms. He would then ask me what was interfering, be it the jaw, tongue, throat, breath flow, etc. I not only use this technique with myself and my students in singing, but in life. When faced with a problem in life, I ask "where is there interference? Where am I holding back, holding on, pushing, pulling, being static?”

Dr. McDonald had a hobby that I didn’t learn about until the last couple of years of his life—collecting, shaping, and polishing found wood. I mentioned to him one day that I felt like we were his pieces of found wood: he would see a shape (hear a voice) and say, “I see the innate beauty in this, and I think I can help it become more smooth and shine even more brightly.” I mentioned that metaphor to him, and it seemed to resonate. He helped me shape and shine my voice, to be sure, but, more than that, helped me become a strong and assured person.

In his final weeks, Annie brought Jim into the living room and we listened to a performance of Schumann’s *Dichterliebe,* which they had presented at IU some years prior. With tears in his eyes, he said, “It’s better than I remember.” That strikes me every time I think of it. How many times in our lives are we in the middle of a beautiful moment that we will cherish looking back on it, but don’t recognize it until later? I think of my time with my mentor with the same fondness.

McD’s legacy is large, and I am grateful to have been a part of it.

"Emily Hindrichs' *Queen of the Night blazed her way like a comet through the role's high tessitura, putting all those tricky triplets in the second part of Der Hölle Rache perfectly in place." (Opera News)*

Emily is currently a soloist with the ensemble of Oper Köln, Germany, and has done many guest engagements in Europe and internationally to great acclaim, appearing with the English National Opera, in Frankfurt, Stuttgart, Chicago, Carnegie Hall, to mention just a few. She was invited to give a recital in Aldeburgh, England, during the Britten Week. Her repertoire includes Mozart, Offenbach, Stravinsky, Zimmerman, Bach, Handel, and the roles of Sophie, Oscar, and Musetta.

Her degree institutions are the University of Southern Mississippi and University of Exeter with a doctorate from New England Conservatory. She was a member of the Seattle Opera Young Artists Program and a Max Kade Scholar in the Middlebury College German for Singers program.

***Emily Hindrichs* writes:**

Jim taught me to differentiate sensation from feeling in my technique—what one feels versus how one feels about it. As a technician this allows me to focus on process rather than result and teaches students the skills necessary for reflecting on their own singing. Beyond that, one is then free to focus on delivering the emotion of the character and the text, unfettered by the inner critic.

He showed great compassion in our lessons. In times of personal difficulty, he would always ask if I wanted to talk or if I wanted to keep working and talk later. I always felt he cared but modeled a clear boundary that let me choose. I try to model this for my students as well.

As a teacher and mentor, Jim was incredibly unselfish. He encouraged me to seek out opinions from other teachers and coaches, and to consider any input I received thoughtfully and with good judgment.

Jim's focus on the "primal sound" let me concentrate on the sound coming out of my body, and taught me to care for it and appreciate it. He never asked me to sound like anyone but me. For that, I am grateful every day.

ACKNOWLEDGEMENTS

Many thanks are given to **Dr. Rachel Eve Holmes,** a gifted and lovely soprano, who gave me permission to include some of her "McDisms" in this book—which are notes she took from the recordings of her voice lessons with James McDonald while studying with him at New England Conservatory and Colorado State University;

... and to **Professor Susan Bender**, University of Wisconsin, Stevens Point, a former Metropolitan Opera Grand Council Auditions winner who studied with James McDonald at the University of Maryland—for being so willing to read this little book and offer much appreciated insights and suggestions;

... and to **Eleanor Shelton**, a published author in her own right and a cherished family friend from our days of living in the Washington, D.C. area—for her expert eyes and thoughtful help in bringing this book to fruition;

... and to **Dr. Leopoldo Erice**, a wonderful pianist from Spain who concertizes internationally and teaches university students in Canada, whom we knew in his student days at Indiana University and in our Middlebury College German courses—for bringing his inquiring mind, generous spirit, and great humor to a review of this book;

... and to **Dr. Veronica Patterson**, Loveland, Colorado's often-published Poet Laureate and wonderful teacher of creative writing—with many and great thanks for her kindness and encouraging help in finding my writing voice at this point in my life, and for being willing to add her insightful thoughts and support to this endeavor;

... and to **Richard Rush**, hospice volunteer extraordinaire, who was a thinking lifeline to Jim in his last months, and an astute and helpful reader of this tribute to Jim's life and teaching. Thank you for all you and Carol do;

... and to former James McDonald voice students—**Josh Whitener, Mark Whitmire, Gordon Hawkins, Susan Bender, Benjamin Czarnota, Rachel Eve Holmes,** and **Emily Hindrichs**—for your caring and thoughtful contributions to this book., which have helped to illuminate the benefits of his teaching beliefs, his own fine character, and his devotion to his students' well-being;

... and to **Stuart and Megan,** our most wonderful children, for their eagle editorial eyes, insightful suggestions, and dedication to their father's legacy in helping me bring this book to life.

And ... to our families, students, and countless friends who so very kindly supported us and our endeavors all the many years Jim and I worked together, sharing our musical muse, from college in 1959 to his passing in 2011 ... **endless thanks.**

AFTERWORD

I've often said that Jim and I were "attached at the hip," for there was never a time in our fifty-one years of togetherness that I was concerned about how or where to connect with him, as our paths always somehow serendipitously crossed.

The first time that happened was eleven months after we married. We had just graduated from Morningside College in Sioux City, Iowa. I went on to summer school at the University of Iowa in Iowa City, to begin my master's degree in organ performance, while Jim stayed in Sioux City to rehearse for the college choir's European tour.

One morning I was feeling rather blue and lonely because I knew that was the day Jim and the choir would be leaving Sioux City on the first leg of their tour and I wouldn't see him again for many weeks. That day, as I was returning to the dorm for lunch (I was a counselor in the nurse's dorm), pushing my bike across the four-lane highway, I stopped at the intersection's median island to wait for the red light to change, but something kept honking, which was puzzling as the light was red and I was safely on the median. Why all the noise I wondered, as I looked up at the big bus in the lane right beside me ... and there in its front window was Jim's smiling face.

I put down my bike, hopped on the bus, waved hello to our many choir friends, gave Jim a quick hug and a kiss, hopped off the bus, stood for a moment watching it go on its way, picked up my bike, ... and my heart sang.

Writing this book has been a lovely adventure as I've become even more aware of what a remarkable man my dear husband was. I'm grateful to have had this opportunity to spend time with his thoughts and his essence of personal integrity, embodied in his life, in his teaching, and in the always thoughtful expression of his gentle, caring nature.

Thank you for sharing this journey with me.